LIVE FROM THE HOMESICK JAMBOREE

WESLEYAN POETRY

LIVE FROM THE
HOMESICK JAMBOREE

ADRIAN BLEVINS

WESLEYAN UNIVERSITY PRESS
MIDDLETOWN, CONNECTICUT

Published by Wesleyan University Press, Middletown, CT 06459

www.wesleyan.edu/wespress

First paperback edition 2013

Printed in the United States of America

ISBN for the paperback edition: 978-0-8195-7461-9

5   4   3   2   1

This project is supported in part by an award from
the National Endowment for the Arts.

NATIONAL
ENDOWMENT
FOR THE ARTS.

A great nation
deserves great art.

Library of Congress Cataloging-in-Publication Data

Blevins, Adrian, 1964–
Live from the Homesick Jamboree / Adrian Blevins.
p. cm. — (Wesleyan poetry)
ISBN 978-0-8195-6930-1 (cloth : alk. paper)
I. Title.
PS3602.L475L58 2009
811'.6—dc22   2009029132

For Weston, Benjamin, and August
and in memory of the father without whom
there would be none of this or us,
Banner Theodore Blevins
1937–2008

The truth is no excuse.

—James Richardson

CONTENTS

LIVE FROM THE HOMESICK JAMBOREE

HOW TO DROWN A WOLF

If your mother's like mine wanting you honeyed and blithe
    you'll get drowned by getting evicted

since the mothers can teach with a dustpan the tons of modes of tossing.

And the fathers will lift your eyes too-early-too-open:
    the fathers can creep up on anything when it's still too wet

to cloister with their weeping and strand you like a seed

or drown at the carnivals with the can-do caroling
    and storefronts and foodstuffs and annulments and Scotch

and off-handed fucking and walking out and moving on

until you've got the drift of wanting a whole river up in you
    and got pretty much the gist

of you needing your crannies hot with a good man's body-silt

until your head is stuffed with a pining for diapers
    and the most minuscule spoons made mostly of silver

and Ajax too and Minwax Oh

in this the dumbstruck story of the American female
    as a shard of terracotta and some driftwood in a dress

while howling at the marrow of the marrow of the bone.

THE HOSPITALITY

It all started when I got the inkling my parents were odd. I mean, after I
could feel it. I mean, after I got the eyes to see I was missing an Easter dress
because I was missing a God because I was watching *All in the Family*
on the trifling TV, though don't say we were lacking in turpentine. Oh,
there were agents for anything we wanted! There was the agent for stripping

and the agent for bonding. There was the agent for cleansing when Mama
washed our records in the sink while she mixed the marinade to douse the beef
and somewhere upstairs Daddy mixed his paints and somewhere downtown
Mama's new boyfriend mixed the finish for some antique and some lawyer's wife
mixed the sugar to the salad for it was the South at the time and we were hot
      were we not

and there was always something to saturate since this was the '70s
when everything was always awash such as the boys on the news in so much blood
the blood somehow left Vietnam to grow over my eye a monocle so magic
that wherever I was I could see everything such as the agent with which my parents
killed the weeds that ravaged the yard and the agent they tossed into the tub

when they were done with the lawn and wanted only to bathe
so they could dress and drink the agents they mixed with the other agents
when the ten or so thousand thirsty men and women came to that house
that was singing almost it was so cordial I mean lethal I mean mannerly okay
and courteous all right and good and decent and sweet.

THE THEATRE PEOPLE

As I remember, they were enormous, like countless cymbals striking,
each one in sickly separation the whole show coming through the door

with me as nothing-but-epidermis in the tub back when I'm nine or ten
bathing during my parents' parties while eyeing the pink robe on the iron hook

since the actors, playwrights, poets, painters, and windfall ass-biters
would always have to pee or vomit or put the lid down and smoke a joint

and *take a breather*, I remember they'd say, while I'd fill up my two palms
and drink the tap water as hot as it would come since I guess that was my medicine

against how much they loathed the war and Phyllis Schlafly and Richard Nixon
and each other if they were breaking up or themselves if they were drunk,

which they were, for I remember tumblers and I remember stumbling: I remember
jingling at the wrists and stretched-out black eyelashes and somehow-hectic
      Capri pants

because even if that wasn't really Anne Sexton in my bathroom swallowing pâté
so she could throw it all up so the pants would fit the next day, it always was

Anne Sexton and Dylan Thomas and their vaporous faces in there
calling me *little girl* and weeping and mumbling and shivering and shaking

until I'd stand up and dry off and stroke their swollen hands
until they were enormous again downstairs with the others singing loud enough

to wake a far-flung neighborhood. Don't wonder why or if the propensity
swelled to other years in other rooms and kinds and types of sticky sex.

This is about the paltry heart that must get gutted sometimes and knotted
and lit-up while sodden. It makes no difference to the story how ample is our fury.

ODE TO THE FISH FRY

I remember how the days seemed never to end, how tacky they got
    at the rim, the sultry residue on the wild roses Mama and everyone

not only didn't wipe off but somehow cultivated with somehow the very breath
    back at the farm when I was a child when everyone left town

to go to what people called anyway "the farm" to sit on porches and be
        intellectual hillbillies
    in peace I guess and drink wine I guess and smoke a little pot maybe

        and play bridge and talk mutiny and riot and insubordination and defiance

and though I've spent my whole life missing the childhood I missed
    while bitching about the fucked-up ways in which the fucked-up bohemians

screwed me over essentially with their atheism and aestheticism
    and tribalism and alcoholism and snooty romanticized Southernism,

somebody needs to write an ode never-the-fuck-the-less
    to the body heat of everyone at the fire pit

        and the hundreds of little fish in a huge bucket in cornmeal
        or flour or something

because there really must be an ode to the body heat of everyone at the pond
    where in the not-quite-dark the fish were caught and reeled in

and thrown up on the bank to be skewered and thrown back into the water
    to be allowed to breathe for a little bit longer on a string

because that froth or foam or whatever that was covering the rhododendron
    and the goldenrod and the rye and all the plants in fact

covered the mothers and the fathers and the brothers and the sisters

as well as that old fort we climbed around in and the huge birch tree
    and the outhouse lilies and the hand pump and the water that trickled from it

as this was before any of us went away and changed and died and such
    and thus it is imperative that some kind of song be sung

about the time before the dread when we liked to stand in a circle
    in the dark around a fire and not know anything and not *say* anything

    but just be there together to just together heed it.

ORIGIN OF THE SPECIES

There's so much happening I wake up running
so of course I sit down and shut my eyes in the so-called library
to think about how every good step forward

is really just a step during which there was no chasm below
though Mama-the-optimist would dispute this
despite her recent stories about a little operation

regarding her gall bladder in a plight she named herself
after searching the Internet, she says, after two years, she says,
of a bothersome, but not fixedly horrendous ache. My mother,

she's happy not to be peeing accidentally in her pants:
she's happy for a certain kind of not-very-fancy-even sherry
that she's happy to drink while she happily makes dinner

while I—I have something lodged in my eye
that says there's a hole in the vessel on which I'm traversing
or maybe a tatty place that's going to rip

or perchance some nefarious people thinking nefarious thoughts about me
in order to set the vessel on fire with their mental ferocity
in order to ruin my chances of surviving the sea

that I didn't even originate because I—I was just a child
in my mother's kitchen, and she—she always had something baking
or boiling in there: she always had the candles lit or let's say

the water, she got it humming, and then when my mother she left
the glassware it broke and spewed across the crosswise sunlight
and I became this vexed I behind a routine face—this obstinate and otherwise I

made just exactly why by what fair and fervent what? By *whom*?

WEANING ELECTRA

She's still sucking on smokes and sticks and the husband's aristocratic cock
    and the roast beef and buttered bread. For when the mother can't love
      the father: for when the mother thinks the father's mad and outrageous

because the father's mad and outrageous (and O the suckling's done and O
    the fat breast departed), the girl-child with the father hair and father eyes
      and his very brainstem and tilt of laughing head

will succumb to her thumb until the thumb is washed in turpentine
    and the mauve coverlet in vinegar since that's what Dr. Spock
      must have said to do in the mid-'60s edition of *Baby and Child Care*

to stop her from sucking on the tips of her fingers and the ends of her his-hair
    though it didn't even work so what was the point since the local boys
      got there soon enough with their own propositions for the purposes

of her mouth. All the same after she was older she sort of liked the hunger
    since it got to the senses like for instance the cinnamon in the tea
      and the keen, keen mountains that were so blue

and sometimes so purple and always so somber-satisfying she couldn't help
    but commence to sucking on the noun and vowel and sentence sounds.
      As if you didn't know this already! As if you weren't yourself

the victim of your own fissures that really must be filled, is what the father said.
Do not cross this burning world hollow and looted, he always said. Not hollow
    and looted, he would say. God darlin' God darlin' God darlin' no.

SCHOOL OF THE ARTS

My father said the most wicked among us were the petty bourgeois
    and the Republicans of the black lakes of all that filched money
      and me sometimes was how it felt

when I was a kid in Daddy's slapdash house of divorce and dejection
    with no way of knowing what kind of girl to be
      and the point is Daddy didn't know either

and wept drunk on the porch because of it sometimes
    until he remembered Rembrandt and Van Gogh
      and woke up the buoyant maestro again

on the sexuality of the Hominid and the evil of the Klan
    and the sway of Dada and the problem of Iran.
      Now Daddy sits in bars in Spain and France

and drinks a beer in Venice and calls on Sunday from Ireland
    to ask me to please tell him in a text or less
      what kind of girl I am

and all I know is soon will come the contagion winter
    and then the winter of the father departed
      and he always promised we'd go fishing.

He would sit in his chair and he would light a cigarette.
    He would curse the starlings for scaring the songbirds
      and cross his heart and hope to die if I would ask him to

and I'm the kind of girl who would always ask him to
    and he would do it and sing about the bones of chickens
      in the bellies of foxes until the gorge got dark

so yes I am about the gist of that darkness and the buoyancy
    of that very particular and faraway backwoods darkness
      when my father would say to go to sleep

and dream anything I wanted like holding your breath
    in a way it was, or like swimming
        like some forever raggedy thing forever underwater.

IN THE ALMOST-EVENING OF ALMOST-CANADA

I'm stripping the paper of iris trailing iris when the word *labia* gets stuck to my labia
    unless it's a vicious recollection of the brimming heads of infants or
        a fat enclave of boys

in the back-when hothouse of no place for kids. By which I mean: they'd say *cunt*
    when they'd need *bitch* because I had followed them around to the back
        of the shack,

I had gestured for the bourbon and I had swigged it—I had swigged and
        I had swallowed
    and was about now to holler how they couldn't say *nigger* and could not also spit

here among the hydrangea of the enterprise of me at fourteen in Virginia
        in the Blue Ridge
    dead set against their hands and hair and tomato-canning Jesus mothers

and the part-leather, part-cloth athletic jackets they seem to want to wed or lick
    and the automotive hi-tech stuff they won't stop talking the knotty virtues of

when what I require is the *Oxford English Dictionary* and a quilt in a meadow
    since I'm nameless between the legs like the sketch of a girl
        splayed out in a meadow

and nameless between the legs like the most minimal sketch in a most
        nominal meadow
    of the general shape of a girl sprayed down horizontal in a frail draft of the vibe

without any real account of what you'd maybe call the inside of the inside
        of the very inside
    when what I've got to say for myself in terms of what I know
        because I remember is this.

NOCTURNE

I was born at high noon in June heaps too early and small
so after the first menses I'd want the darkling opposite.
All I mean is, the night was everything back then

though obviously I was a mom. Always at Goodwill
in the fiendish afternoon while pretending to look for boy shirts
and boy pants and backpacks, I'd search out the night

in the shape of a black cape or sweater or tablecloth
with the eyes of little witches painted on. It's how
the babies showed up in the first place with their high screams

and daylight requirements—it was my time of great ignorance
and I wanted to correct it—it was imperative that I shed
the limpidness and decency that covered me at each fiery opening

slit. That's why I'd let some boy be conveyed through the night
through what was called my body: he'd take me down with him
via some vegetated shack of a supposed bed while I'd shut my eyes

against the very idea and ordeal of him and think I believe about
the haybales out there and the marsupials snooping for little meats
to bite and chew or bury in black holes I thought went down forever

to the other side of the earth where there were bound to be bees
sputtering pollen on what I'm sure I knew was every single
sweet and flaxen thing I remain in my rigidity too medieval to name.

FIRST FALL IN MAINE

Before we place the vein blue sheetrock against the stud walls
and invite the brawny boys to take out their ballpeen hammers
and their measuring sticks: before the men start cursing the job

in order to pass the time is my experience and to prove they're men

I want to say how I can't even find my own heart in this house.
It must be stowed away in the basement or under the winter clothes
inside some storage boxes beside the furnace. I can't find anything

less than a heart around here, either. I went looking for a cocktail

and couldn't find the shot glass. I went wanting my childhood,
and it wasn't in the medicine chest. No, it wasn't in the wardrobe,
but there were sandals—leather ones with thin straps I may have worn

to a wedding or to one of those lawn parties they have back home

with girls in wide-brimmed straw hats and skirts that twirl.
I might remember a banquet, dulcimer music, and a bouquet
of flowers, but couldn't that be a little pre-dawn wishful-thinking reverie?

Listen to how hard the rain keeps on coming down! I could depict

the leaves falling in big blobs of coffee-colored mini-splotches,
but instead of the umbrellas and the fleece and the ponchos I need
I've got the baby teeth of my three kids in little bags in the middle drawer

of my dresser. I've got someone's dried-out umbilical cord stored there,

too. But there's no lute music in the meadow because there is
no meadow left. There is no necklace or locket or reaping-season jig.
Just this shedding of the fucking lot, and the long wait for the mend.

LIVE FROM THE HOMESICK JAMBOREE

Here in the province of Fuck You we're really in the province of Fuck Me
    since I hate my head since it involves my mouth

and hence the talk expressing no acquaintance with New England winter crops
    or how to make a stew that's not my mother's soup

or find any other way to disobey both parents vis-à-vis the homeland they're so high on
    because the mountains are not flat is how they like to put it

when the real reason is Daniel Boone invading our hometown in 1767
    and calling it Wolf Hills to commemorate the massacre

of the pack that ate his dogs. Daniel Boone's in other words
    the real reason my parents are not recovered from being from home

and the real reason I'm not recovered unless the actual predicament here
    is just myself being myself and my husband being my husband

nine hundred miles away from where the tea is customarily sugared
    and the dogwoods start blooming at the end of March

causing a delectable whiteness to pervade the atmosphere
    and though the dogwood is a tree and trees should not be eaten,

the dogwood seems anyway to want to be devoured
    since here in the district of The Gone Astray

I want to devour everything transformed by my distance
    into yet another elegy, since what I really don't get

is what made Boone think the trouble and the hunger would stop
    when he got his rifle and bent into the snarl and shot.

NOVELETTE

With her one horrid eye persistently unfastened, a vigilant bird
watched my grandfather during The Great Depression
use each evening of one whole year to wander his corn fields
knowing this world is just one pig after another

in one pen after another. Therefore, the bird heard him suppose,
shouldn't he with his best gun, machete, Buick, or rope
terminate his acquaintance with the tiresome set-up
of breakfast-lunch-dinner-dawn-dusk-fall-winter-spring-summer-

blah-blah-blah? But his girls were good-looking
and made such fine pies, so the bird watched him live wretchedly
until he died more naturally of cancer
too soon to see his people become the dopefiends, doctor-haters,

masturbators, insomniacs, sleep fanatics, shut-ins, and teetotalers
the bird knew they would become, for the purpose of girls
is to just ruin everything with wanton reproduction
so that now now now it's really relentless—how heavy

his people got in their limbs and how torrential, thus,
the frenziedly wind, though beyond the eye of the bird
is the small, ashen brain of the bird, and below that, a heart,
I swear, through which come the iffy notes of this cruel song.

BIG RAIN DAY

A drunkard and womanizer they say of him, a mean little man
and a fuck-up and a slacker and a liar with a head that's turning to ash
and a heart that's turning to trash and trash, in fact, from the base
of a putrid cask with his name carved in it like he hadn't been rocked,
like there was not enough milk, like we hadn't wept when we heard
he was coming, like we hadn't cried when he got here, like we
didn't know what sassafras he was, like he wasn't hot and shining.
Actually when he was born all of us inhaled implausibly in chorus
like we were a gang of sentry flowers in the same russet basket
and this went on for a long time while he learned to walk and talk
and read about the bear in the boots and the sleepwalking billygoat
and now he's going from bar to bar in Tennessee like a godamned idiot
like he hadn't been *bathed*, like he was not sung to and praised,
and while it's true this wrong isn't like those carried out against
the people who loved the boys who went down in Saigon and Iraq,
it's still a hideous turn of events even if one of us was meant
to jangle around solitary in the hinterlands, to stagger about
looking for maybe his soul in a novel twilight filled with a million
not-novel bottles of Bud and we don't think that's right, that doesn't sound
like us, call us crazy but that whole way of thinking is entirely incorrect
in terms of what we'd imagine we'd be doing in two thousand and seven
in godforsaken America the fucking beautiful, so hey you off-course little brother,
you depraved little fucker, you goddamned big heartache and big rain day
and big VIP of our feels-like-impending catastrophe: this is an urgent message
sort of like a prayer in song-code to you from us saying please cancel
the shambles somehow and grit your teeth and just, somehow, *stop*:
where you're taking us the quiet's too quiet and the dark too dark.

COUNTRY SONG

The rednecks are loathsome I know
maybe because they've hardly been anywhere or
because they don't wonder if there's a God or
because they're too busy wearing boots
the ends of which could be knives and cotton t-shirts
the sleeves of which maybe they think were invented
to wrap cigarettes in and hair that's so short
it's imperceptible to coordinate with the heart
that's attached essentially to the truck the redneck
can't ever get enough of maybe because the wheels
      are big and enduring I guess so anyway
if you're in love with a redneck it's easy to wake in a sweat
seeing him rub his Chevy with the one silky finger
or open his mouth to lick persuasively the hood adornment
and beyond the fact that nobody should suck the horns
of even dreamt rams there's the actual problem of personhood
and it's a big one I know maybe because

      inside the redneck somewhere is a man

and even if he wouldn't care to discotheque

or dye his hair the color of a flash

or take you for one little day to the Museum of Modern Art

or commence to playing you the flute

or baking you a Lady Baltimore cake like in the John Cheever story

or even say *Cheever* even on his deathbed,

      a man is a composite of nerves and thirst
sort of like a long valley of birds and a man is a pelt
filled to the rim with the feathers of geese and I'm sorry but
you must forgive him even while you hate him, you must

smack him yes I will admit but meanwhile
please gather him up because never in the world before

was anything so hammered.

SEMANTIC RELATIONS

Though naturally I love them they are a monstrosity, acute and unruly,
already pig-headed on the way from the airport to come and infect me

with what kind of mayonnaise is better than Hellmann's and which of us
got the new bike versus who crashed the old and who's drinking too much

versus who ought to get the special Weight-Watchers brownies
and who isn't on that plan but really should be and whose kid is in what university

versus whose kid is in which other. Yes I love them but they talk
        too much about nothing
because they are after pulling me out of the stillness I came up North for

because in their opinion I've always been too faraway
starting in the '70s like an anonymous planet up in my room

while they all sat around downstairs vehement on the topic
of everything I was missing because after all it was just the *hearth*—

just the kids pouring juice and telling jokes while the scant one upstairs
plotted some wraithlike escape like could she become some kind of particle?

Could she float out to sea maybe on a raft of splintered pillars?
This is part of the story of my people who won't say much

but rigorously chatter about global warming and formaldehyde and cancer
and Hemingway and Peter Jennings and Bush who we despise

because he is a killer. My people are not killers—they are romantics—
they like to sit around on porches and tell false stories

because lies are more agreeable than me eyeing them haughtily and saying
as a matter of fact, though I'm forced to do it because we're almost out

of time, O my high-hilled, prattling sweethearts—O my brothers and sisters
of hoodwink and swindle and fiddle and twaddle and drivel and hokum and tripe.

POEM FOR MY DAUGHTER AUGUST
DISPARAGING THE GOSSAMER DEPICTIONS
OF THE WOMEN OF CERTAIN SOUTHERN TEXTS

*For this is the country . . . where girls wear organdy and batiste and eyelet embroidery and no panties
on account of the climate and have smooth little faces to break your heart and when the wind of the
car's speed lifts up their hair at the temples you see the sweet little beads of perspiration nestling there,
and they sit low in the seat with their little spines crooked and their bent knees high toward the dash-
board and not too close together for the cool, if you could call it that, from the hood ventilator.*
                                                                    —ROBERT PENN WARREN

Since it's true the women not only of the South but probably all over
    dole out iced tea in books while they slowly thrust off their blue panties
        and do things in the kitchen with pasta and herbs and nuts and oils
           while removing their hair from nets
              likened to those in the boats of fishermen

and are thus the hot blue yonder in a tribute to the mothers
    these men of the South and elsewhere didn't get
        but were hysterical for and so evoked as girlfriends and wives
           in aprons near the clothesline
              and in gardens with their hair all up

but coming down while humming low-slung tunes
    while cleaning out the sullied barrels within which they keep
        clothes-pins maybe and white washing rags,
           I feel I ought to walk around the neighborhood
              spying on the women here

to summon them in groups at the river with their washing boards
      and at quilting bees
with babies in slings talking home remedies. Oh August and Everyone:
    since the girls are always in some mode of surrender:
        since they're always being overcome
           by the warring sounds in words like *truck* and *ax*

as well as the truck itself and the ax itself while somehow meanwhile sparkling,
    maybe I should just go on and devote myself to the rivers
        and to all the bodies of water the women are said to be like
            such as the ocean on my left and the ocean on my right
                and the creeks back home

in the blue series of hills I-swear-to-God called Arcadia
    where we used to camp sometimes and where I threw up
        my first Southern Comfort while a series of boys
            tried to get me to live with them
                in cabins they wanted to build themselves

out of the stones of the creek beds because despite being illiterate
    they wanted the combination of Ruby and Ada in *Cold Mountain*
        because in addition to glistening they wanted ginseng
            because they wanted a girl
                who could tame and slaughter and store and trade

the products of the barns and the fields
    with their hair all up but coming down against dresses also nimbly-rainy
        and blue panties that exist in order to be eliminated
            in that period of time
                when twilight bounds softly forth on the grass

two or three poems over in the anthology from that other suddenly-I-realized-moment
    about how in comparison to the droppings of last year's horses
        we are ever so much cower and shrivel and grovel and weep
            and squander and fritter and waste. And since look I guess I've done it
            since look I guess there's a lot of water here

and women everywhere stripped while plodding, I guess I should be content.
    But since you must never in your farmhouse my darling
        weep into your pillow upstairs and because
            you must never my darling celebrate the bees making honey
              without knowing too how they wither off

to the side of the hive, I am for the sake of the truth and for the sake of
    your future self
  and for your brothers too turning now to a depiction of women
    as arid and heady and defiant and uncouth
      so you might remember me as forthright and honest
        and turning and turning now

to a depiction of the seeing eye unwrapped and the unbeautiful mouth
  spectacularly unbolted, for I am talking witchcraft here
    because I am versus the folklore though I know it's tender
    and therefore versus the fathers
      who never once laid themselves down

in what they'd call the tall reed grasses to conjure you up
  out of a yawning lode of shadow and plasma
    to carry for you and for your brothers and for all I know for the Lord
    the old burden although it is a splendor
      and the hindrance and the weight.

FIRST WINTER IN MAINE

As regards my recent silence there was just too much to say.
Yes I mean the forest of late summer becoming the forest of fall
becoming the charismatic forest of mute and callous intent.

O yes I mean the snow forest becoming the *first* forest
just beyond the glass door we put there deliberately
to stare at the trees that have nothing at all to say, if you're willing

to listen: just the branch going down and some kind of lion
rising—just the fox and raccoon looking hard with me looking back
with just my boys in my head since they're gazelles by disposition

who won't be protected from any aspect of the forest
but must stand smack-dab in the middle of the wreck
that isn't the wreck of the weather, but the wilder, harder wreck

of the missing father and abstracted mother that's the hard-line wreck
of the hard-listening inside that by disposition and genetics
will lean them against the pine and alder and snow birch

for six seven eight nine months of whatever we are when we lock our mouths
to mourn our losses from the insides of our jackets and black wool caps
with just our eyes in our faces and the lungs in our chests

in the flabbergasted shut up of sucking and sucking and sucking it in.

WHY THE MARRIAGE FAILED

From the beginning it was the money, how we would not or could not make it.
It was never avarice, I resent the implication, it was how much like starlings
children are with those same raggedy screechings and us such languid nest makers:
him with his camera pointed up and me in the chair with the Plath in my lap.

From the beginning it was our innocence, it was our impertinence, it was
      a bent outhouse
in the dead dead double-dead clot of twisted winter. It was him with the black cloth
over his shoulders and that huge camera for a face and my face also like an infant's
in the photos he made. It was stupidity and I don't mind saying it, for
      we were farcical,

we were illogical, we were like a circle spinning and just that hollow—
we were the fragrance of the idea of the meaning of not. We didn't want destruction,
we were totally against that, so we made it our philosophy: we sought
a garden of Black-eyed Susans because all we wanted was to frolic

because like everyone else, we just wanted to be happy. But we were too wet,
we were like fog, we were an orchard of water in a cabin, stupor gone amuck.
We'd sit on the porch and look for some fields to farm, but we were too fertile
and didn't have hoes. We were minus a measuring cup and missing an umbrella

when you two boys got here and that was it, we were history. There were maybe
three candies in our pockets, but we weren't blank, we were stuffed
from loving you—we'd stare at your craving mini-mouths mid-shriek and go
oh my god how entirely exquisite oh my god what have we done.

FIRSTBORN

He was the wound who slithered through the wound I hadn't known was there.
He was a slur, he was wet: he was enormously inarticulate. Hairless and desolate

was he: in love with himself was he, he, he! Was he a ravenous, toothless snake

in a small pelt sheath? Was he a dragon, was he a fawn? His cloistered bones
were made of stars and his tiny eyes were tiny stars: my cunt-his-starship

was now, however, a lion: we couldn't say which of us was roaring more.

O Mother, I saw robins there, as it was March. O Mother it was March
when he devoured me. Or maybe that's erroneous and what happened was

he got a will. Maybe what happened was he opened his eyes for the milk to swill

to swell those bones until *he* was the tower and he the lion. I'd watch at midnight
for incisors. He'd call at midnight to say there was Budweiser there

and girls in short-shorts: there were grottos there, and into the grottos

he would slink. O Mother, what animal or spirit is he? O Mother,
from whence could it come—from whence did he come—but me?

MORNING SONG

I didn't *really* think I knew everything and the husband
not. I didn't really care what kind of skillet one made
the omelet in. No, all I frankly wanted was for him
to know to stroke and settle me, such was my shock
at the birth of that child. Oh, such was my distress!
It was like I was walking on bits of sunny glass
down some dowdy highway after a twilight crash.
Or had been severed in two with an ax. And had thereafter
to put the top half of me in a tree and the other half
low like underwater. And my eyes had been gouged out
by the horns of goats. And everyone's voice
had little landscaping stones in it and the eggs were always black
now that wood was plastic and the vacuum puffed out
rather than in little murky swarms of when he-the-baby
would crawl and he-the-baby would walk and oh
he-the-baby this and he-the-baby *that*! People! I didn't like it.
And couldn't imagine how I'd ever endure the world.
Since it could take him from us. And us from him.
World of a heap of poisons. World of spiders and snakes.
World of war. World of crush and gorge. Why couldn't
the husband have predicted it? Why hadn't he stopped us?
World of idiots! World of the inexcusably dippy and daft!

JESUS SAVES

The coal-hauling train car said Hi *Loretta, Jesus Saves* in white-chalk, ardent letters.
So do the bathroom stalls and bumper stickers riding their diesels up Highway 81
and the letters Nate's mom sends in the blue envelopes she adores

because they are sacred—they are great—they are from The Christ Store of Baltimore.
I used to think it was boredom; I believe I thought the paperback Jesus
        of the droopy eyes
came to those who had nobody to love but the good-times Jesus of the afterlife picnic,

but it's a prayer, isn't it, Loretta? It's what we want instead of what we've got—
not the dead little boy in the dining room with his heart and lungs pierced
by a kitchen knife: not the mother-face weeping while opening the drawer

or the mother-face drafting the suicide note while the not-dead-yet little boy
wondered where was the yogurt or tried to strap his tongue around the nouns
that describe a world of bees and bananas unfurled in the grass to eat and toss.

Don't cry, maybe he said before it was too late, but she was too busy killing him
to hear anything but the hurricane of killing him and by then anyway
there was not-rain everywhere and a kind of humming he couldn't name

and somewhere low down, Loretta, not rage or pain, but wonder that he was
        going to be
a plume instead of a boy and waft around his beautiful haunt-mother
        in a perpetual mew
like this blue-eyed, billboard Jesus—this hot potato, wacky Jesus—

        saving who, Loretta, *who?*

The dead soldier boy's photo makes me think *oh his poor mother*
as though he'd never been an actual person with fingers etcetera

but the mother's right eye shredded by hundreds of pieces of flying pink glass
or the mother's malignant lung reduced to cinders in the infirmary furnace.

It's wrong to think of dead people as appendages, so as the dirge persists
I try to comprehend that the boy will never use his spicy mouth again

or promenade the lamplight streets because his Mama won't stop ragging him
about always being so negative thinking the cup's half-empty.

But because the cup is more than half-empty *now*—
because once you're dead the cup is no longer even a cup

unless it's a poltergeist cup your poltergeist mother will have to perch on her head
now that her hands have been amputated and her legs set on fire—

that's wrong, too. It is just so wrong of me not to know what to
        call the paraphernalia
the boys are given to extinguish the women inside them

by killing off the women inside the others, but I don't have that kind
        of dictionary here
and not even you with your magnificent heart can save me now.

For Tony

CV RIDER

As to the particulars of her know-how, here's an addendum
made of the she who pushed out the Cro-Magnons
and carried them across foul-smelling gardens
and served up the brew for five bucks a table
to buy meat at Winn Dixie that she'd then slice and broil
and place on chipped plates she got from the thrift stores
to which she became addicted because there are blankets there too
and anything can be disinfected and hung out to dry
and spread across the Cro-Magnons she is herein broadcasting
she fed and cleaned and cooled and heated
in order to advance to a little Homo sapien with flash cards
she designed and cut and drew and nature walks
intent on the nouns the babies forever crave because
their mouths are blank and you're a shit if you don't fill them
with all there is to love and hate like *banana* and *vomit* and *mother*
and *father*. Only when the father turns up confused and then missing
can you take out the verbs, which she needs you to know
she flung out day after day and year after year because
what good is a father with no *say goodbye* to go with him?
Everyone's got an adventure; everyone's driving to El Dorado
for just one example and setting up get-aways and tagging on
triumphs, but what about the escapade of staying at a standstill
and saying *spider*, saying *star*, saying: look, *child*, look?

DREAM IN WHICH I FIND MYSELF CONFRONTED
YET AGAIN WITH WHY THE MARRIAGE FAILED

Always there are squabbles and fussings over assets. The difficulty in this dream was water. Because while our neighbor had the good mind to build his house by the river, my own husband was a slipshod tropical forest who dawdled his life away singing and playing throw-stone with the children. The children were handsome, but thirsty. Their mouths dried up like peaches in dust storms and so they almost always got the almost-always-fatal diseases until they commenced their affairs with the neighbor's idiot daughter, who in addition to being stupid was the most doting girl in the land. She made my boys lemonade and bathed them at night with water perfumed in lavender. She sewed my boys britches with needles she dipped in blood and picked fine lettuces she grew with seeds she germinated in her belly and hence concocted a salad some said could sing, as their father so beautifully did. I loved that bad man, their father. When he walked in the woods the birds would land on his hands. And he always saw deer swimming in the stars or other intact mammals lying in pockets of grass with their eyes as big as planets. But he was impossibly *frolicsome*, their father. He was more like a woodchuck than a man. I mean, I called him Cinderella. I mean, when I said at last that I was going to cut my own throat to get reborn by some feral river or lake so my boys would never leave me again for stupid, magic, crazy, whorish, doting girls, he showed me the pennies he kept in his mouth and swallowed each one so tenderly down.

DEAR NEW MOTHERS OF AMERICA

As for living to one side of yourself like a pile of rice
    in the vicinity of the fish (as for being an eye-self
        hanging above a body-self

content with separating cowboy stuff
    from G.I. Joe stuff from Batman boxer shorts):
        yeah, I've been there, I know what you mean,

don't get me started. There were, in fact,
    ten rooms in one house.
        And dust and a couch and dirt and lamps.

I was thus the body of the two hands
    and the body of the feet
        becoming somehow

the body primarily of the mouth
    demanding bleach. It's not that I was
        pitiful. It was more like:

who else would eradicate
    the rotten scattering of skin flakes
        and hair and spiders

and such? Who else would swab the spit?
    So sure it was wholesome at the river
        when I was a new mom

but creepy is the point
    to live for the wiping of boots
        and the soaking of jackets

with my mouth open and my poor tongue sticking out
    like I was hoping to comprehend
        what was wrong

with being mostly as I say
      just the eye part of something
         soaking in the grimy particles

while all the other girls went on being actual girls
      and I'm sorry to have to say this
         since I know it's upsetting

but that's the way it was; I appreciate your asking
      come again real soon
         be careful watch your step.

WHY THE MARRIAGE FAILED II

If he could say anything he'd say the catastrophe was me and my heinous ways:
he'd say me standing in the yard cross-eyed with the rake. Mostly the inward eye

he would say if he were drunk or stoned enough since he'd say the library
since he'd say me driving away even during ice storms since what he'd
      really want to say

would be the willfulness that was in the case of me to him a little pilfering maybe
of his manliness. On the one hand isn't she interesting he would say, and couldn't she

keep a party going. But on the other: why couldn't she just keep her mouth shut
and where's her cotton dress. I don't blame him being as he is from North Carolina.

But then again: did he or did he not sit with my father in the smoky den talking
Harmonious Bosch? Something's wrong with the whole phrase *heinous ways* anyway

since I didn't kill anybody, since all I did was just be insolent, since if it was organic
it got on my nerves, since I hated walking since I hated the forest since I hated nature

since if it wasn't budding it was dying and putrid seeing how you had to walk
      on trees limbs
all the time. Sure I could've thought *firewood* or *vitamins and minerals for the dirt,*

but I didn't have on the right shoes since we were always so broke and anyway
I had to spread a crib sheet over the picnic table and line up the meat and put
      the two babies

in their seats. I had to find the forks and knives and wipe them off with the
      finale of my shirt.
Meanwhile he'd be shooting something with his camera. He'd be oozing and aching

over a robin's nest or putting his light meter to the bark of a tree. And maybe
      he'd even be singing
in spite of the squirrel bodies and the bodies of the birds that had dropped
      to the ground

and in the particular case of my own body, that was another thing he had
        nothing to say about
except where was it when it was standing in the yard cross-eyed with the rake?

And where was it when it was in the library thirty miles down the old
        Lee Highway?
And all I'm saying is: that is a very good question, why don't you
        engrave the answer

on some fibrous object like a wasp's nest and send it to me parcel post
from wherever you are across whatever sea doing whatever you do in paradise?

DEAR READER

IS IT JUST ME or am I COOKING now? HONEY-CHILD,
DON'T BELIEVE A WORD OF IT. I can't drink champagne
and artichokes give me earaches. Even the herb garden
is OVER AND DONE WITH. It's a WASTE OF TIME
and a PAIN IN THE ASS. Who cares about PARLSEY, SAGE,
ROSEMARY, AND THYME? Why are there TOO MANY COOKS
IN THE KITCHEN and thunderstorms and moths and bridges
and monkeys and shoes? WHAT'S THE DEAL with fishing lures
and why aren't there enough HOURS IN THE DAY? Why does Terry Gross
have to say FRESH AIR the way she does? What is WRONG
WITH HER? She should be BEATEN WITHIN AN INCH
OF HER LIFE. She should be SHOT. I have really got SOME ISSUES
with Terry Gross. Terry Gross REALLY THINKS SHE'S HOT.
Everyone thinks they are REALLY HOT: they are driving hot cars;
they are buying hot beds; they are jumping up and down on the sidewalks
going HOT, HOT, HOT. Even *him*—even *he* thinks he's hot;
he walks LIKE A GIRL; he shops at the co-op; he peeks in on Elizabeth,
who has always thought she was REALLY, REALLY HOT.
I'm asking you this: who cares about the apricot? Does he really eat
free-range chickens? And why won't his canoe sink? I'VE GOT A LOT
ON MY MIND; I'm worried ALL THE TIME. I've got a migraine,
an appointment with the dermatologist, and NO TIME TO KILL.
My mother-in-law is a JESUS FREAK. She's a WALKING ADVERTISEMENT
for Jesus. Well, MAYBE SHE'S RIGHT. Maybe THAT'S THE WAY
TO GO. Maybe Jesus is hotter than anyone, A HOT-TAMALE
and HOT-TO-TROT. Maybe Jesus ought to come down here right now
and SHOW ME A THING OR TWO. What would he do? DRAW ME
A BATH OR MAKE ME A CAKE? I would do something: I would
undress him. I would relieve him of his robe. I would get out my camera
and TAKE A PICTURE and send it RIGHT ON DOWN THE LINE to you.

HEY YOU

Back when my head like an egg in a nest
was vowel-keen and dawdling, I shed my slick beautiful
and put it in a basket and laid it barefaced at the river
among the taxing rocks. My beautiful was all hush
and glitter. It was too moist to grasp. My beautiful
had no tongue with which to lick—no discernable
wallowing gnaw. It was really a breed of destruction
like a nick in a knife. It was a notch in the works
or a wound like a bell in a fat iron mess. My beautiful
was a drink too sopping to haul up and swig!
Therefore with the trees watching and the beavers abiding
I tossed my beautiful down at the waterway against
the screwball rocks. Even then there was no hum.
My beautiful was never ill-bred enough, no matter what
you say. If you want my blue yes everlasting, try my
she, instead. Try the why not of my low down,
Sugar, my windswept and wrecked.

THE SECOND MARRIAGE

I should be skinning rabbits or memorizing Tolstoy:
one of the kids needs a tetanus shot and we're all out

of eggs and bread. But here I am on the bathroom floor
heeding Emmylou laud her man on the hi-fi

with a big, fat copy of *Vogue* on my lap.
Out in the boondocks in blue jeans and T-shirts

I could halt a low-grade crisis
like four cows breaching the borders of a fence

while moaning vis-à-vis the creepy strain
of their unmilked teats. But him saying

I looked like a field hand that night at the dinner party
(half drunk on red wine) has brought me here

to the nerve center of the tinsel
where women dip themselves in lavender-misted Vaseline

and roll around in a vat of dyed sugar
because we are to glitter like lilacs under lace—

we are to float—we are to glisten at the core of the briar patch
because they are the briar patch

and we are the festooned highjinks
that is the feminine generosity, Amen, Amen, Amen.

SIN CITY

I've got to know everything or I'll fail as a person, so of course I watched
the Triple X DVD with my husband, who's jumbo-electric-frenetic-feral
even when he's trying to stop me from wasting money on the telephone's
        Star-69 feature

because I am altogether lethargy and he's up at dawn even on the weekends
because he is the reincarnation of the founding fathers
and I won't even mop the kitchen floor during the weeks he's flying
        all over the country

making a ton of money I admit I merrily use for murky purposes like Ritz dye,
which is good for changing an off-blue jacket into a burgundy one,
which is good for whiling the time away while he's gone making all that money

I'd make myself if someone would just hire me, though in addition to being lazy
I'm so crazy I take out my heart and measure it with a plastic green ruler,
and, while he's grilling kabobs and installing dimmer switches
        and tasting the garden soil

to gauge how much pH must be added, announce suddenly in the garage,
where in addition to grilling he's designing a workbench and an opera
        for Martin guitars,
that I am megawatts in The Benevolence Category

because if there's one thing I won't do it's make the same mistake twice,
referring to the divorce, and for this reason I'll watch Sin City with him,
though he's got to promise the kids won't catch us and answer
        any question I posit

regarding the erections of the cameramen and the pain of the putting in
        of the clit rings.
But now I can't stop worrying about Delray of the ceramic bowl breasts
that could not move to accommodate Brick's tongue, which I'm guessing

from the look of that sugar-white scar must have been slashed all-but-in-half
by the inmate who must've taught him that pitiless thump-thump-thumping trick
I fear will infect Delray's insides with a malignancy that'll cause her eggs to rupture

and her poor Mama to die forlorn in a nursing home from the lack of baby slaver
     and baby cluck
that is the only viable hereafter if you are a sinner like she is a sinner
     and I am a sinner,
though God knows this time I'm giving virtue a shot.

HOW WE TALK

Is he sticks his shoes out from under the bed like ten warring bullets in a row
    until I have to move them as they impede the vacuum
        and more upsettingly pierce my delicate eye.

Also how we talk is not during the making of dinner that I blatant forsake
    since food is fattening and just another means by which he infuses
        the house with clatter
    until I'm not kidding when I say I can't think

and have to walk around all day hating the Bush Administration until
        he's forced to defend it
    not because he doesn't also hate it but because that way I guess he thinks
        he'll get more drama or maybe because he wants to restrict my scorn

since he doesn't want me to be so critical since maybe he's afraid one day
        it'll be his turn
    and he's walking on air of late by which I guess I mean he's fragile
        unless I'm the one who's fragile

        and going therefore in and going therefore in

since I don't like it out here in the hypothetical real world and for the record
        never did
    including this house we're living in that takes too long to clean
        with his shoes in it impeding the vacuum that I don't like either

and therefore don't use because it's too domestic and wrecks the Gemini side of me
    that wants everything to just fly apart so I can tell what it's made of
        or at least spit on it or catch it on fire with my lighter.

Consequently for the record how I feel about how I feel is mainly just
        exceedingly aggrieved
    by the unruly domestic residue of also his hats and jackets and festering barbells
        and so on ad infinitum sitting weedy and unheeded in front of us

such as his disappointment at how I'm turning out because I'm not
the most effective wife or mother or even person given how much I smoke
and smoke and fret and vex about how his shoes etcetera

do if you're wondering somehow mutilate poor old errant me.

THE WAY SHE FIGURED HE FIGURED IT

You get over these constant storms and learn to be married all over again, every day.
　　　　　　　　　　　　　　　　　　　—BARRY HANNAH

The foyer is hers because the kettle is hers as it was made for water
　　　　and the water is hers
　　　because the sac that grew the baby was hers though the semen
　　　　　　that made the sac was his
　　　　　　　like his boots are his and the tea that's of the kettle

after it enters his mouth is his unless it's hers since it's inside the kitchen that's hers

and therefore not his unless he's simmering the Asian sauces that are his
　　　　because they're dense and knotty rather than milkish and paltry
　　　　　　　like everything else from the nation state of the motherland

of the no-mercy child who won't stop sucking and wanting and whining
　　　　in the ear that is his

although the child herself belongs somehow to the woman and thus
　　　　its hunger is hers
　　　as is the bed and dresser and mirror and latch
　　　　　　though the hammer naturally is his and the saw and lumber

and back and muscle he suffered to build because he guessed he thought it would be

good for something besides this house like a pestilence of people who weren't his
　　　　because nothing was his except the whirl he carried in his belly of the mix-up
　　　　　　of loving her in the first place

like being sucked into a burrow of lava embers and putting your tongue to
　　　　it until it caught fire

and all he could say was that the burn was his—this hole in the mouth—
　　　　this fiasco of the woman bent now in the garden to smell the cilantro
　　　　　　as though she didn't know his head was split

with hating her and loving her and hating her and loving her

because she was an ache and a kink and somehow the furrow—the groove
    and the rut—
      and age and death and kiss and fuck and not-fuck and song and not-song
      and no it was not sweet though he'd go on and carry it

           since also—since mostly—it was.

IF THE UNIVERSE SENDS ME A GRIP

I'll drop my Ajax and say something else, but this is about how
my full-to-bursting motherliness—my pasty yield to the sweaty troops
of me and the dad in the bed and me and me all-milky with the rainy children
in the bed—was not stupidity and was not psychosis

no matter what the braincases thought back then

since like everyone else they've got to die and hover in the milieu,
making now more actually about how the saints are going to exonerate
        even the braincases

since like everyone else they're fragments of salt and the dust of fish:

ghoul spit on the thigh with a real life to lose but no human honeycomb in a crib
to float around at midnight and not-lick but near-lick

since the divine stillness of a child is the very death-defiance motherhood
        is all about

since it's impossible but not really but *maybe* given how now is in point of fact
the waning time of me going in the opposite direction of full-to-bursting
since I'm too old to grow a baby and moreover too wary to scatter myself
        to microscopic pieces
like I had all the time in the world. And the money and the grit.
        The cockamamie lovingness.

THE WANING

When you're sixteen with pristine nipples it's hard to imagine
    you'll go a little bit blind one morning years later trying to read a bottle,
        but in point of fact you'll be standing in the shower

in early fall in Maine at 43, the water will be brisk and zesty,
    and though the hair-washing process will still be to put the shampoo in
        and take the shampoo out, you'll have on this day

a big desire for a little naked and rainy English, a question about
        the syntactical schemes
    of the manufacturers of certain bathing products, and like
        your back-then change of heart for Larry

and his cigs you won't always smoke and his hair you won't always stroke,
    there will be on this fall day in Maine at 43 a shifting of the receptiveness
        thanks to a sudden dulling-out of the eye

like someone put a smudge in you or took away your scanty organs
    to amend them in formaldehyde or lacquer or gasoline or Tide
        when what you think should be sentence fragments about how to wash your hair

look like far away Japanese drawings of piles of rocks instead. O, back before
    the gore, before you were covered in ejaculate, before your cells got Xeroxed
        and your body was milk and you were roughly the odor of something

wafting like a cantaloupe, why didn't you get off that blanket in that dumb garden
    and do a little jig in honor of all the faculties such as you could see and you
        could walk? You could touch your nose with the tip of your tongue!

You could dive, you loved the river, your hair was silken, your skin magnificent.
    O, it wouldn't last forever, why were you so ignorant, you squandered it,
        you let fly the splendor, you unacquainted little wench, you mess, you error.

THE IMPERATIVE SENTENCE

For God's sake wash the windows and stop being so arctic-hearted.
Exercise some and avoid the various sugars. Avoid the sugar of sunshine

with a hat, and the sugar of revenge by kneeling down on your knees
and asking the gods to transform you into the kind of person

who would eagerly shelter the unenlightened boogies walking your neighborhood
with eyes as grave as graves under snow. Avoid the sugar of indifference

by never forgetting your allergy medicine and thus avoid your afternoon
headache, which is where the cold cells of your arctic heart go thump, thump,

thump. Or just forget your head completely, for nobody ever got happy
on his or her head. Burn the philosophers' leather-bound books

and make a lemon pie and have sex in the kitchen and sing *Hey Diddle Diddle*
twice at dawn and please stop smoking. Make a list of all your enemies

and send them little things in the mail. Send A the kind words you sometimes felt
but never said. Tell A she is fierce. Send B a real wedding band and C

some baby clothes and maybe a silver whistle. Send D a spring wind
that when he opens the envelope will blow the whole, dire past kaput.

Send your mother-in-law pictures of her grandchild swinging on a swing,
send unknown bankers fresh fives and tens from the money machine.

And send your old employers some poems! But be sure to *write* the poems first—
the poems of forgiveness avoiding the sugar of sullenness and the sugar of smite

that you will make once you learn to duck the sugar of impatience
by sitting quietly in the dark and doing nothing for a long time at all.

NOW THERE'S A RIVER

Death to the savage little bitch that I was. Death to her fringe and to her pie.
Death not to the memory so much of her long blonde hair, but death
to how and why she tossed it. Death to that skinny, infantile idiot's idiocy,
death to her lesser breasts. Death to Skynard's freebird and every last
Firebird, death to the dogwood under which she'd sulk. Death to Scarlet-the-prototype,
death to the theory and practice of the black velvet dress. Not and never death

to the South—no!—but death to some of its women and more of its men—

death to the handkerchief, death to the crystal vase and bitten lip and silk slip
and tittle-tattle time of tea. Death to the bow tie. Death to Washington and Lee!
Death to the football game, death to the boys' jerseys and tires—death to their fingers
and dicks—death to that icy girl's icy piccolo: death to her legendary silver barrette
and the old mahogany dressing table on which it lay, death to her curling iron
and most categorically now on the Kennebec at the start of the summer

of her forty-fourth year, wild-hell-and-smash death to her heart that was bone.

ACKNOWLEDGMENTS

I am grateful to the editors who first published many of the poems in this collection, most in earlier versions.

American Poetry Review, "Dear Mothers of America," "How We Talk," "Morning Song," "Ode to the Fish Fry," "The Way She Figured He Figured It." *Beloit Poetry Journal*, "Why the Marriage Failed." *Café Review*, "Watching the News Hour," "The Second Marriage." *Chattahoochee Review*, "Why the Marriage Failed II," "If the Universe Sends Me a Grip." *Court Green*, "The Hospitality." *88: A Journal of Contemporary American Poetry*, "Jesus Saves," "Firstborn." *Georgia Review*, "Now There's a River." *H_N_G_M_N*, "Dear Reader" (as "Exercise in the Pitch of Shrill"). *North American Review*, "Weaning Electra." *Pleiades*, "First Winter in Maine." *Ploughshares*, "Country Song," "The Waning." *Poetry*, "Novelette," "How to Drown a Wolf" (as "How to Cook a Wolf"). *Slate*, "Poem for my Daughter August Disparaging the Gossamer Depictions of the Women of Certain Southern Texts." *Smartish Pace*, "Hey You," "The Origin of the Species." *TriQuarterly*, "Semantic Relations," "The Theatre People," "Sin City." "Hey You" also appeared on *Poetry Daily* (www.poems. com).

"Why the Marriage Failed" received a Special Mention, *Best of the Small Presses*, 2007. It also appears in *From the Fishouse: An Anthology of Poems that Sing, Rhyme, Resound, Syncopate, Alliterate, and Just Plain Sound Great*, Dungy, O'Donnell, and Thomson, Editors.

Special thanks to Colby College for the sabbatical that gave me the time to finish this book. I am also grateful to the Rona Jaffe Foundation, the Kingsley Tufts Poetry Awards, and the Sewanee Writers' Conference for their encouragement. Thanks to Patrick Donnelly, Peter Harris, Tony Hoagland, Susan Kenny, Tilar Mazzeo, Ira Sadoff, Chase Twichell, and Nate Rudy for help with poems along the way. Finally, thanks to Suzanna Tamminen for her miraculous foresight and assistance—this book would not exist without her.

NOTES

The epigraph is from James Richardson's *Vectors: Aphorisms and Ten-Second Essays*, Ausable Press, 2001.

The first line of "Country Song" is borrowed from August Kleinzahler's "The Wind in March," from *Red Sauce, Whisky, and Snow*, Noonday Press, 1996.

The first half of the first line of "Why the Marriage Failed" is from Gerald Stern's "Cost," from *This Time: New and Selected Poems*, W. W. Norton & Company, 1999.

The epigraph introducing "Poem for my Daughter August Disparaging the Gossamer Depictions of the Women of Certain Southern Texts" is from Robert Penn Warren's *All the King's Men*.

ABOUT THE AUTHOR

Adrian Blevins's *The Brass Girl Brouhaha* won the 2004 Kate Tufts Discovery Award. Blevins is also the recipient of a Rona Jaffe Writer's Foundation Award, a Bright Hill Press Chapbook Award for *The Man Who Went out for Cigarettes*, and the Lamar York Prize for Nonficiton. Blevins teaches at Colby College, in Waterville, Maine.

CPSIA information can be obtained at www.ICGtesting.com
Printed in the USA
BVOW07s1225040913

330042BV00001BA/16/P

9 780819 574619